# Keys to
# The
# Deeper
# Life

# Keys to The Deeper Life

## A.W. Tozer

### Revised and Expanded

CLARION CLASSICS
Zondervan Publishing House
Grand Rapids, Michigan

KEYS TO THE DEEPER LIFE

*Clarion Classics* are published by the
Zondervan Publishing House
1415 Lake Drive, S.E., Grand Rapids, Michigan 49506

**Library of Congress Cataloging-in-Publication Data**

Tozer, A. W. (Aiden Wilson), 1897–1963.
  Keys to the deeper life / by A. W. Tozer. — Rev. and expanded. p.
cm.
  Rev. ed. of: Leaning into the wind. 1984.
  ISBN 0-310-33361-X
  Spiritual life. I. Tozer, A. W. (Aiden Wilson), 1897–1963. Leaning
into the wind. II. Title.
  BV4501.2.T669 1988
  248.4—dc19
                                                        88–14901
                                                            CIP

Scripture quotations are taken from the King James Version.

*Designed by Kim Koning*

Printed in the United States of America

90  91  92  93  94  95  96 / DP / 34  33  32  31  30  29  28

For some time it has been evident that we evangelicals have been failing to avail ourselves of the deeper riches of grace that lie in the purposes of God for us. As a consequence, we have been suffering greatly, even tragically. One blessed treasure we have missed is the right to possess the gifts of the Spirit as set forth in such fullness and clarity in the New Testament.

A. W. Tozer

# Contents

# Contents

# Introduction

In every age God chooses unique men and women through whom He speaks to the world at large. A. W. Tozer was such a man in his day. Now a quarter of a century after his death, his legend lives on, and in many ways more vividly than ever.

Tozer was not a prolific writer. He labored over what he wrote. But he was published widely in the religious periodicals of his day—that is, when editors could prevail upon him to write.

He wrote as sparingly as he spoke. Everything he wrote, as well as much of what he said, was lean, precise, often cryptic, but always spiritually insightful. A graphic model of the author himself.

Probably the most prolific outpouring of Tozer's writings appeared in the *Alliance Weekly* (not the *Alliance Witness*). He edited the paper, the official publication of The Christian and Missionary Alliance, for ten years. Each issue opened with an editorial by him, by all odds the most read single feature appearing in that publication or indeed, possibly in any other Christian publication during the period of his editorship.

To see him at work writing was to destroy any image of the distinguished pastor, renowned lecturer, or highly respected denominational leader that he was.

Tozer usually worked at a desk with a gooseneck lamp. He wore a green eyeshade much like the prototype of the cigar-chomping newspaper editor of his day. Shunning his coat, he worked in a vest with rubber bands on his arms at the elbow to pull up his shirt sleeves.

Plainly, Tozer was a thinker. His sermons were no more usual than his writings. It is probably a truism to say that Tozer was not a popular speaker in the general sense of the word. His audiences, however, did appreciate what he had to say.

It is also probably correct to say that in most of the churches that he pastored, the predominance was represented by blue-collar people. Yet he could speak to their needs just as well as he could titillate minds of the intelligentsia on university campuses, where he was frequently invited by Inter-Varsity Christian Fellowship groups.

On the other hand, no one could ever accuse Tozer of tailoring his message to please his audience. In fact, many felt that he did exactly the opposite.

A case in point is the time he was invited to speak at the annual conference of the Christian Writers

Institute in Chicago. Having heard of his predilection to speak the truth as he saw it, I, as conference director, suggested to him that the purpose of these sessions was to encourage beginning writers to perfect their techniques. Looking away from me, he nodded affirmatively in an absent sort of way. This was my first experience in inviting him to speak, so I was quite unprepared for the results: a blistering attack on Christian writers who ignorantly assumed that Christian fiction was a valid means of communicating the truths of Jesus Christ.

His exact words I do not remember, but the idea was simply that fiction was false, a perpetrator of error and hence totally beneath the high art of Christian writing.

I do not know what I said at the close of his address. I do know that I attempted to minimize its effect on the astonished writers who had been subject to the diatribe.

Tozer could be as harsh and vitriolic in his writing as he occasionally was in his speaking. Probably the most notable example of this was his editorial in the *Alliance Weekly* criticizing an expanded translation of the Book of Romans by a well-known scholar, then instructor at Moody Bible Institute.

Whatever else he had to say about the book I do not recall. One phrase, however, ignited controversy throughout the entire evangelical community. Reading the book, opined Tozer, was like trying to "shave with a banana."

To his credit, Tozer later repented of his brash statement. He made public apology in the editorial columns of the *Alliance Weekly*—but only for the unkind cut, not for his evaluation of the book.

Tozer was a deeply committed man. Anyone who knew him realized this. Although he might not have been considered a theologian in the strictest sense, he applied the truths of Scripture to what he spoke, wrote, and lived to the best of his ability. He was also a very private man. The people who knew him well, knew him principally on the spiritual level.

He always was glad to talk with people who had spiritual problems. That is, provided they remained objective and did not get into maudlin subjects.

Praying with Tozer was a unique experience. I was delighted the first time he invited me to join him in his study for a time of prayer. After discussing some portion of Scripture over which he recently had been meditating, he suggested we pray. As a much younger man, I waited to see what posture he would take in order that I might comply.

To my surprise he rose from his chair and stepped to the middle of his study and knelt down. I did the same. There, kneeling erect with no chair or table for support, we prayed facing one another for the next half hour. Thinking back now, I recall clearly that the physical feat involved in the spiritual exercise left no room for mental woolgathering.

In conversation also, following Tozer's line of thought involved paying strict attention to what he was saying. He appeared to choose his words as carefully in casual conversation as he did in speaking from the pulpit and writing.

It may come as a surprise to some to realize Tozer is credited with nineteen books. As is true of most authors, some achieved greater success than others. The astonishing fact is that they are more popular today than when he was alive.

By far the most popular is *Pursuit of God*. It was this title that first projected him into the limelight of the general evangelical Christian public as an author with a pertinent message for the day and with a style different from his contemporaries. It was followed by *Root of the Righteous*, which also received high acclaim during his lifetime. Now, two decades after his death, other titles are enjoying a revival of public attention.

For all of us who have appreciated Tozer as a man, revered him as a writer, and acknowledge him as "a prophet in our time," today's renaissance of interest in Tozer comes as a long overdue accolade to a true man of God.

Robert Walker, editor
*Christian Life*

# Preface

The material that follows comes from a series of articles that first appeared in *Christian Life* magazine. They were published more than a quarter of a century ago in the emerging days of the renewal of interest in the person and work of the Holy Spirit. At that time they established a biblical basis for the recognition of the renewal by the evangelical community. As they captured the essence of this phenomenon for the world of Tozer's time, uniquely also they speak to us as the voice of God in our day.

For additional insight into the mind and heart of a man to whom God was speaking three decades ago, see the Addendum for an interview conducted with Tozer. It appeared in the August 1954 issue of *Christian Life* magazine and is as contemporary in its insights today as it was then.

# ONE

# Leaning into the Wind

Wherever Christians meet these days one word is sure to be heard constantly repeated; that word is *revival*.

In sermon, song and prayer we are forever reminding the Lord and each other that what we must have to solve all our spiritual problems is a "mighty, old-time revival." The religious press, too, has largely gone over to the proposition that revival is the one great need of the hour, and anyone who is capable of preparing a brief for revival is sure to find many editors who will publish it.

So strongly is the breeze blowing for revival that scarcely anyone appears to have the discernment or the courage to turn around and lean into the wind, even though the truth may easily lie in that direction. Religion has its vogues very much as do philosophy, politics and women's fashions. Historically the major world religions have had their periods of decline and recovery, and those recoveries are bluntly called revivals by the annalists.

Let us not forget that in some lands Islam is now enjoying a revival, and the latest report from Japan indicates that after a brief eclipse following World War II Shintoism is making a remarkable come-back. In our own country Roman Catholicism as well as liberal Protestantism is moving forward at such a rate that the word "revival" is almost necessary to describe the phenomenon. And this without any perceptible elevation of the moral standards of its devotees.

A religion, even popular Christianity, could enjoy a boom altogether divorced from the transforming power of the Holy Spirit and so leave the church of the next generation worse off than it would have been if the boom had never occurred. I believe that the imperative need of the day is not simply revival, but a radical reformation that will go to the root of our moral and spiritual maladies and deal with causes rather than with consequences, with the disease rather than with symptoms.

It is my considered opinion that under the present circumstances we do not want revival at all. A widespread revival of the kind of Christianity we know today in America might prove to be a moral tragedy from which we would not recover in a hundred years.

Here are my reasons. A generation ago, as a reaction from Higher Criticism and its offspring, Modernism, there arose in Protestantism a powerful movement in defense of the historic Christian faith. This, for obvious reasons, came to be known as Fundamentalism. It was a more or less spontaneous movement without much organization, but its purpose wherever it appeared was the same: to stay "the rising tide of negation" in Christian theology and to restate and defend the basic doctrines of New Testament Christianity. This much is history.

### Falls Victim to Its Virtues

What is generally overlooked is that Fundamentalism, as it spread throughout the various denominations and nondenominational groups, fell victim to its own virtues. The Word died in the hands of its friends. Verbal inspiration, for instance (a doctrine which I have always held and do now hold), soon became afflicted with *rigor mortis*. The voice of the prophet was silenced and the scribe captured the minds of the faithful. In large areas the religious imagination withered. An unofficial hierarchy decided what Christians were to believe. Not the Scriptures, but what the scribe thought the Scriptures meant became the Christian creed. Christian colleges, seminaries, Bible institutes, Bible conferences, popular Bible expositors all joined to promote the cult of textualism. The system of extreme dispensationalism which was devised, relieved the Christian of repentance, obedience and cross-carry-ing in any other than the most formal sense. Whole sections of the New Testament were taken from the church and disposed of after a rigid system of "dividing the Word of truth."

All this resulted in a religious mentality inimical to the true faith of Christ. A kind of cold mist settled over Fundamentalism. Below, the terrain was familiar. This was New Testament Christianity, to be sure. The basic doctrines of the Bible were there, but the climate was just not favorable to the sweet fruits of the Spirit.

The whole mood was different from that of the Early Church and of the great souls who suffered and sang and worshiped in the centuries past. The doctrines were sound but something vital was missing. The tree of correct doctrine was never allowed to blossom. The voice of the turtle [dove] was rarely heard in the land; instead, the parrot sat on his artificial perch and dutifully repeated what he had been taught and the whole emotional tone was somber and dull. Faith, a mighty, vitalizing doctrine in the mouths of the apostles, became in the mouth of the scribe another thing altogether and power went from it. As the letter triumphed, the Spirit withdrew and textualism ruled supreme. It was the time of the believer's Babylonian captivity.

In the interest of accuracy it should be said that this was a general condition only. Certainly there were some even in those low times whose longing hearts were better theologians than their teachers were. These pressed on to a fullness and power unknown to the rest. But they were not many and the odds were too great; they could not dispel the mist that hung over the land.

The error of textualism is not doctrinal. It is far more subtle than that and much more difficult to discover, but its effects are just as deadly. Not its theological beliefs are at fault, but its assumptions.

It assumes, for instance, that if we have the word for a thing we have the thing itself. If it is in the Bible, it is in us. If we have the doctrine, we have the experience. If something was true of Paul it is of necessity true of us because we accept Paul's epistles as divinely inspired. The Bible tells us how to be saved, but *textualism goes on to make it tell us that we are saved*, something which in the very nature of things it cannot do. Assurance of individual salvation is thus no more than a logical conclusion drawn from doctrinal premises, and the resultant experience wholly mental.

### Revolt from Mental Tyranny

Then came the revolt. The human mind can endure textualism just so long before it seeks a way of escape. So, quietly and quite unaware that any revolt was taking place, the masses of Fundamentalism reacted, not from the teaching of the Bible but from the mental tyranny of the scribes. With the recklessness of drowning men they fought their way up for air and struck out blindly for greater freedom of thought and for the emotional satisfaction their natures demanded and their teachers denied them.

The result over the last 20 years has been a religious debauch hardly equaled since Israel worshiped the golden calf. Of us Bible Christians it may truthfully be said that we "sat down to eat and to drink, and rose up to play." The separating line between the Church and the world has been all but obliterated.

Aside from a few of the grosser sins, the sins of the unregenerated world are now approved by a shocking number of professedly "born-again" Christians, and copied eagerly. Young Christians take as their models the rankest kind of worldlings and try to be as much like them as possible. Religious leaders have adopted the techniques of the advertisers; boasting, baiting, and shameless exaggerating are now carried on as a normal procedure in church work. The moral climate is not that of the New Testament, but that of Hollywood and Broadway.

Most evangelicals no longer initiate; they imitate, and the world is their model. The holy faith of our fathers has in many places been made a form of entertainment, and the appalling thing is that all this has been fed down to the masses from the top.

That note of protest which began with the New Testament and which was always heard loudest when the Church was most powerful has been successfully silenced. The radical element in testimony and life that once made Christians hated by the world is missing from present-day evangelicalism. Christians were once revolutionists—moral, not political—but we have lost our revolutionary character. It is no longer either dangerous or costly to be a Christian. Grace has become not free, but cheap. We are busy these days proving to the world that they can have all the benefits of the gospel without any inconvenience to their customary way of life. It's "all this, and heaven too."

This description of modern Christianity, while not universally applicable, is yet true of an overwhelming majority of present-day Christians. For this reason it is useless for large companies of believers to spend long hours begging God to send revival. Unless we intend to reform we may as well not pray. Unless praying men have the insight and faith to amend their whole way of life to conform to the New Testament pattern there can be no true revival.

### When Praying Is Wrong

Sometimes praying is not only useless, it is wrong. Here is an example: Israel had been defeated at Ai, and "Joshua rent his clothes, and fell to the earth upon his face before the ark of the Lord until the eventide, he and the elders of Israel, and put dust upon their heads."

According to our modern philosophy of revival this was the thing to do and, if continued long enough should certainly have persuaded God and brought the blessing. But "the Lord said unto Joshua, Get thee up; wherefore liest thou upon thy face? Israel hath sinned, and they have also transgressed my covenant which I commanded them. . . .

Up, sanctify the people, and say, Sanctify your-
selves against to morrow; for thus saith the Lord
God of Israel. There is an accursed thing in the
midst of thee, O Israel: thou canst not stand before
thine enemies, until ye take away the accursed thing
from among you."

We must have a reformation within the Church.
To beg for a flood of blessing to come upon a
backslidden and disobedient Church is to waste
time and effort. A new wave of religious interest
will do no more than add numbers to the churches
that have no intention to own the Lordship of Jesus
and come under obedience to His commandments.
God is not interested in increasing church atten-
dance unless those who attend amend their ways
and begin to live holy lives.

Once the Lord through the mouth of the prophet
Isaiah said a word that should settle this thing
forever: "To what purpose is the multitude of your
sacrifices unto me? saith the Lord: I am full of the
burnt offerings of rams, and the fat of fed beasts; and
I delight not in the blood of bullocks, or of lambs, or
of he goats. When ye come to appear before me, who
hath required this at your hand, to tread my courts?
Bring no more vain oblations; incense is an abomi-
nation unto me; the new moons and sabbaths, the
calling of assemblies, I cannot away with; it is
iniquity, even the solemn meeting. . . . Wash you,
make you clean; put away the evil of your doings
from before mine eyes; cease to do evil; learn to do
well; seek judgment, relieve the oppressed, judge

the fatherless, plead for the widow.... If ye be willing and obedient, ye shall eat the good of the land."

Prayer for revival will prevail when it is accompanied by radical amendment of life; not before. All-night prayer meetings that are not preceded by practical repentance may actually be displeasing to God. "To obey is better than sacrifice."

We must return to New Testament Christianity, not in creed only but in complete manner of life as well. Separation, obedience, humility, simplicity, gravity, self-control, modesty, cross-bearing: these all must again be made a living part of the total Christian concept and be carried out in everyday conduct. We must cleanse the temple of the hucksters and the money changers and come fully under the authority of our risen Lord once more. And this applies to this writer as well as to everyone that names the name of Jesus. Then we can pray with confidence and expect true revival to follow.

If we are alert enough to hear God's voice we must not content ourselves with merely "believing" it. . . . Commands are to be obeyed, and until we have obeyed them we have done exactly nothing at all about them. And to have heard them and not obeyed them is infinitely worse than never to have heard them at all.

**A. W. Tozer**

# TWO

# Panting
# after
# God

Suppose some angelic being who had since creation known the deep, still rapture of dwelling in the divine Presence would appear on earth and live awhile among us Christians. Don't you imagine he might be astonished at what he saw?

He might, for instance, wonder how we can be contented with our poor, commonplace level of spiritual experience. In our hands, after all, is a message from God not only inviting us into His holy fellowship but also giving us detailed instructions about how to get there. After feasting on the bliss of intimate communion with God how could such a being understand the casual, easily satisfied spirit which characterizes most evangelicals today? And if our hypothetical being knew such blazing souls as

Moses, David, Isaiah, Paul, John, Stephen, Augustine, Rolle, Rutherford, Newton, Brainerd and Faber, he might logically conclude that 20th century Christians had misunderstood some vital doctrine of the faith somewhere and had stopped short of a true acquaintance with God.

What if he sat in on the daily sessions of an average Bible conference and noted the extravagant claims we Christians make for ourselves as believers in Christ and compared them with our actual spiritual experiences? He would surely conclude that there was a serious contradiction between what we think we are and what we are in reality. The bold claims that we are sons of God, that we are risen with Christ and seated with Him in heavenly places, that we are indwelt by the life-giving Spirit, that we are members of the body of Christ and children of the new creation, are negated by our attitudes, our behavior and, most of all, by our lack of fervor and by the absence of a spirit of worship within us.

Perhaps if our heavenly visitor pointed out the great disparity between our doctrinal beliefs and our lives, he might be dismissed with a smiling explanation that it is but the normal difference between our sure standing and our variable state. Certainly then, he would be appalled that as beings once made in the image of God we could allow ourselves thus to play with words and trifle with our own souls.

Significant, isn't it, that of all who hold the evangelical position those Christians who lay the greatest store by Paul are often the least Pauline in spirit. There is a vast and important difference between a Pauline creed and a Pauline life. Some of us who have for years sympathetically observed the Christian scene feel constrained to paraphrase the words of the dying queen and cry out, "O Paul! Paul! What evils have been committed in thy name." Tens of thousands of believers who pride themselves on their understanding of Romans and Ephesians cannot conceal the sharp spiritual contradiction that exists between their hearts and the heart of Paul.

That difference may be stated this way: Paul was a seeker and a finder and a seeker still. They seek and find and seek no more. After "accepting" Christ they tend to substitute logic for life and doctrine for experience.

For them the truth becomes a veil to hide the face of God; for Paul it was a door into His very Presence. Paul's spirit was that of the loving explorer. He was a prospector among the hills of God searching for the gold of personal spiritual acquaintance. Many today stand by Paul's doctrine who will not follow him in his passionate yearning for divine reality. Can these be said to be Pauline in any but the most nominal sense?

### If Paul Were Preaching Today

With the words "That I may know him" Paul answered the whining claims of the flesh and raced on toward perfection. All gain he counted loss for the excellency of the knowledge of Christ Jesus the

Lord, and if to know Him better meant suffering or even death it was all one to Paul. To him conformity to Christ was cheap at any price. He panted after God as the heart pants after the waterbrook, and calm reason had little to do with the way he felt.

Indeed a score of cautious and ignoble excuses might have been advanced to slow him down, and we have heard them all. "Watch out for your health," a prudent friend warns. "There is danger that you will become mentally unbalanced," says another. "You'll get a reputation for being an extremist," cries a third, and a sober Bible teacher with more theology than thirst hurries to assure him that there is nothing more to seek. "You are accepted in the beloved," he says, "and blessed with all spiritual blessings in heavenly places in Christ. What more do you want? You have only to believe and to wait for the day of His triumph."

So Paul would be exhorted if he lived among us today, for so in substance have I heard the holy aspirations of the saints damped down and smothered as they leaped up to meet God in an increasing degree of intimacy. But knowing Paul as we do, it is safe to assume that he would ignore this low counsel of expediency and press onward toward the mark for the prize of the high calling of God in Christ Jesus. And we do well to follow him.

When the apostle cries "That I may know him," he uses the word *know* not in its intellectual but in its experiential sense. We must look for the meaning—not to the mind but to the heart. Theological knowledge is knowledge about God. While this is indispensable it is not sufficient. It bears the same relation to man's spiritual need as a well does to the need of his physical body. It is not the rock-lined pit for which the dusty traveler longs, but the sweet, cool water that flows up from it. It is not intellectual knowledge about God that quenches man's ancient heart-thirst, but the very Person and Presence of God Himself. These come to us through Christian doctrine, but they are more than doctrine. Christian truth is designed to lead us to God, not to serve as a substitute for God.

### A New Yearning Among Evangelicals

Within the hearts of a growing number of evangelicals in recent days has arisen a new yearning after an above-average spiritual experience. Yet the greater number still shy away from it and raise objections that evidence misunderstanding or fear or plain unbelief. They point to the neurotic, the psychotic, the pseudo-Christian cultist and the intemperate fanatic, and lump them all together without discrimination as followers of the "deeper life."

While this is of course completely preposterous, the fact that such confusion exists obliges those who advocate the Spirit-filled life to define their terms and explain their position. Just what, then, do we mean? And what are we advocating?

For myself, I am reverently concerned that I teach nothing but Christ crucified. For me to accept a teaching or even an emphasis, I must be persuaded that it is scriptural and altogether apostolic in spirit and temper. And it must be in full harmony with the best in the historic church and in the tradition marked by the finest devotional works, the sweetest and most radiant hymnody and the loftiest experiences revealed in Christian biography.

It must lie within the pattern of truth that gave us such saintly souls as Bernard of Clairvaux, John of the Cross, Molnos, Nicholas of Cusa, John Fletcher, David Brainerd, Reginald Heber, Evan Roberts, General Booth and a host of other like souls who, while they were less gifted and lesser known, constitute what Dr. Paul S. Rees (in another context) calls "the seed of survival." And his term is apt, for it was such extraordinary Christians as these who saved Christianity from collapsing under the sheer weight of the spiritual mediocrity it was compelled to carry.

To speak of the "deeper life" is not to speak of anything deeper than simple New Testament religion. Rather it is to insist that believers explore the depth of the Christian evangel for those riches it surely contains but which we are as surely missing. The "deeper life" is deeper only because the average Christian life is tragically shallow.

They who advocate the deeper life today might compare unfavorably with almost any of the Christians that surrounded Paul or Peter in early times. While they may not as yet have made much progress, their faces are toward the light and they are beckoning us on. It is hard to see how we can justify our refusal to heed their call.

What the deeper life advocates are telling us is that we should press on to enjoy in personal inward experience the exalted privileges that are ours in Christ Jesus; that we should insist upon tasting the sweetness of internal worship in spirit as well as in truth; that to reach this ideal we should if necessary push beyond our contented brethren and bring upon ourselves whatever opposition may follow as a result.

### That I May Perfectly Love Thee and Worthily Praise Thee

The author of the celebrated devotional work, *The Cloud of Unknowing*, begins his little book with a prayer that expresses the spirit of the deeper life teaching "God, unto whom all hearts be open ... and unto whom no secret thing is hid, I beseech Thee so for to cleanse the intent of mine heart with the unspeakable gift of Thy grace, that I may perfectly love Thee and worthily praise Thee. Amen."

Who that is truly born of the Spirit, unless he has been prejudiced by wrong teaching, can object to such a thorough cleansing of the heart as will enable him perfectly to love God and worthily to praise Him? Yet this is exactly what we mean when we speak about the "deeper life" experience. Only we mean that it should be literally fulfilled within the heart, not merely accepted by the head.

Nicephorus, a father of the Eastern Church, in a little treatise on the Spirit-filled life, begins with a call that sounds strange to us only because we have been for so long accustomed to following Jesus afar off and to living among a people that follow Him afar off. "You, who desire to capture the wondrous divine illumination of our Savior Jesus Christ—who seek to feel the divine fire in your heart—who strive to sense and experience the feeling of reconciliation with God—who, in order to unearth the treasure buried in the field of your heart and to gain possession of it, have renounced everything worldly—who desire the candles of our souls to burn brightly even now, and who for this purpose have renounced all the world—who wish by conscious experience to know and to receive the kingdom of heaven existing within you—come and I will impart to you the science of eternal heavenly life—"

Such quotations as these might easily be multiplied till they filled half a dozen volumes. This yearning after God has never completely died in any generation. Always there were some who scorned the low paths and insisted upon walking the high road of spiritual perfection. Yet, strangely enough, that word perfection never meant a spiritual terminal point nor a state of purity that made watchfulness and prayer unnecessary. Exactly the opposite was true.

### Hearing But Not Obeying

It has been the unanimous testimony of the greatest Christian souls that the nearer they drew to

God the more acute became their consciousness of
sin and their sense of personal unworthiness. The
purest souls never knew how pure they were and
the greatest saints never guessed that they were
great. The very thought that they were good or great
would have been rejected by them as a temptation of
the devil.

They were so engrossed with gazing upon the face
of God that they spent scare a moment looking at
themselves. They were suspended in that sweet
paradox of spiritual awareness where they *knew*
that they were clean through the blood of the Lamb
and yet *felt* that they deserved only death and hell
as their just reward. This feeling is strong in the
writings of Paul and is found also in almost all
devotional books and among the greatest and most
loved hymns.

The quality of evangelical Christianity must be
greatly improved if the present unusual interest in
religion is not to leave the church worse off than she
was before the phenomenon emerged. If we listen I
believe we will hear the Lord say to us what He once
said to Joshua, "Arise, go over this Jordan, thou, and
all this people, unto the land which I do give to
them, even to the children of Israel." Or we will
hear the writer to the Hebrews say, "Therefore,
leaving the first principles of the doctrine of Christ,
let us go on unto perfection." And surely we will
hear Paul exhort us to "be filled with the Spirit."

If we are alert enough to hear God's voice we must
not content ourselves with merely "believing" it.

How can any man believe a command? Commands
are to be obeyed, and until we have obeyed them we
have done exactly nothing at all about them. And to
have heard them and not obeyed them is infinitely
worse than never to have heard them at all, especially in the light of Christ's soon return and the
judgment to come.

If ... your soul cries out to God, for the living God, and your dry and empty heart despairs of living a normal Christian life ... then I ask you: Is your desire all absorbing? Is it the biggest thing in your life? ... If your heart cries "Yes" to the questions you may be on your way to a spiritual breakthrough that will transform your whole life.

A. W. Tozer

# THREE

# Showered with His Gifts

"Concerning spiritual gifts, brethren," wrote Paul to the Corinthians, "I would not have you ignorant."

Certainly Paul meant nothing derogatory by this. Rather, he was expressing a charitable concern that his fellow believers should be neither uninformed nor in error about a truth so vastly important as this one.

For some time it has been evident that we evangelicals have been failing to avail ourselves of the deeper riches of grace that lie in the purposes of God for us. As a consequence, we have been suffering greatly, even tragically. One blessed treasure we have missed is the right to possess the gifts of the Spirit as set forth in such fullness and clarity in the New Testament.

Before proceeding further, however, I want to make it plain that I have had no change of mind about the matter. What I write here has been my faith for many years. No recent spiritual experience has altered my beliefs in any way. I merely bring together truths which I have held during my entire public ministry and have preached with a fair degree of consistency where and when I felt my hearers could receive them.

In their attitude toward the gifts of the Spirit Christians over the last few years have tended to divide themselves into three groups.

First, there are those who magnify the gifts of the Spirit until they can see little else.

Second, there are those who deny that the gifts of the Spirit are intended for the Church in this period of her history.

Third, there are those who appear to be thoroughly bored with the whole thing and do not care to discuss it.

More recently we have become aware of another group, so few in number as scarcely to call for classification. It consists of those who want to know the truth about the Spirit's gifts and to experience whatever God has for them within the context of sound New Testament faith. It is for these that this is written.

### What Is the True Church?

Every spiritual problem is at bottom theological. Its solution will depend upon the teaching of the

Holy Scriptures plus a correct understanding of that teaching. That correct understanding constitutes a spiritual philosophy, that is, a viewpoint, a high vantage ground from which the whole landscape may be seen at once, each detail appearing in its proper relation to everything else. Once such a vantage ground is gained, we are in a position to evaluate any teaching or interpretation that is offered us in the name of truth.

A proper understanding of the gifts of the Spirit in the Church must depend upon a right concept of the nature of the Church. The gift problem cannot be isolated from the larger question and settled by itself.

The true Church is a spiritual phenomenon appearing in human society and intermingling with it to some degree but differing from it sharply in certain vital characteristics. It is composed of regenerated persons who differ from other human beings in that they have a superior kind of life imparted to them at the time of their inward renewal.

They are children of God in a sense not true of any other created beings.

Their origin is divine and their citizenship is in heaven.

They worship God in the Spirit, rejoice in Jesus Christ and have no confidence in the flesh.

They constitute a chosen generation, a royal priesthood, a holy nation, a peculiar people.

They have espoused the cause of a rejected and crucified Man Who claimed to be God and Who has pledged His sacred honor that He will prepare a place for them in His Father's house and return again to conduct them there with rejoicing.

In the meantime they carry His cross, suffer whatever indignities men may heap upon them for His sake, act as His ambassadors and do good to all men in His name.

They steadfastly believe that they will share His triumph, and for this reason they are perfectly willing to share His rejection by a society that does not understand them.

And they have no hard feelings—only charity and compassion and a strong desire that all men may come to repentance and be reconciled to God.

This is a fair summary of one aspect of New Testament teaching about the Church. But another truth more revealing and significant to those seeking information about the gifts of the Spirit is that the Church is a spiritual body, an organic entity united by the life that dwells within it.

### Each Member Joined Together

Each member is joined to the whole by a relationship of life. As a man's soul may be said to be the life of his body, so the indwelling Spirit is the life of the Church.

The idea that the Church is the body of Christ is not an erroneous one, resulting from the pressing too far of a mere figure of speech. The apostle Paul in three of his epistles sets forth this truth in such sobriety of tone and fullness of detail as to preclude the notion that he is employing a casual figure of speech not intended to be taken too literally.

The clear, emphatic teaching of the great apostle is that Christ is the Head of the Church which is His body. The parallel is drawn carefully and continued through long passages. Conclusions are drawn from the doctrine and certain moral conduct is made to depend upon it.

As a normal man consists of a body with various obedient members with a head to direct them, so the true Church is a body, individual Christians being the members and Christ the Head.

The mind works through the members of the body, using them to fulfill its intelligent purposes. Paul speaks of the foot, the hand, the ear, the eye as being members of the body, each with its proper but limited function; but it is the Spirit that worketh in them (1 Cor. 12:1–31).

The teaching that the church is the body of Christ in 1 Corinthians 12 follows a listing of certain spiritual gifts and reveals the necessity for those gifts.

The intelligent head can work only as it has at its command organs designed for various tasks. It is the mind that sees, but it must have an eye to see through. It is the mind that hears, but it cannot hear without an ear.

And so with all the varied members which are the instruments by means of which the mind moves into the external world to carry out its plans.

As all man's work is done by his mind, so the

work of the church is done by the Spirit, and by Him alone. But to work He must set in the body certain members with abilities specifically created to act as media through which the Spirit can flow toward ordained ends. That, in brief, is the philosophy of the gifts of the Spirit.

## How Many Gifts?

It is usually said that there are nine gifts of the Spirit. (I suppose because Paul lists nine in 1 Corinthians 12.) Actually Paul mentions no less than 17 (1 Cor. 12:4–11, 27–31; Rom. 12:3–8; Eph. 4:7–11). And these are not natural talents merely, but gifts imparted by the Holy Spirit to fit the believer for his place in the body of Christ. They are like pipes on a great organ, permitting the musician wide scope and range to produce music of the finest quality. But they are, I repeat, more than talents. They are spiritual gifts.

Natural talents enable a man to work within the field of nature; but through the body of Christ God is doing an eternal work above and beyond the realm of fallen nature. This requires supernatural working.

Religious work can be done by natural men without the gifts of the Spirit, and it can be done well and skillfully. But work designed for eternity can only be done by the eternal Spirit. No work has eternity in it unless it is done by the Spirit through gifts. He has Himself implanted in the souls of redeemed men.

For a generation certain evangelical teachers have

told us that the gifts of the Spirit ceased at the death of the apostles or at the completion of the New Testament. This, of course, is a doctrine without a syllable of biblical authority back of it. Its advocates must accept full responsibility for thus manipulating the Word of God.

The result of this erroneous teaching is that spiritually gifted persons are ominously few among us. When we so desperately need leaders with the gift of discernment, for instance, we do not have them and are compelled to fall back upon the techniques of the world.

This frightening hour calls aloud for men with the gift of prophetic insight. Instead we have men who conduct surveys, polls and panel discussions.

We need men with the gift of knowledge. In their place we have men with scholarship—nothing more.

Thus we may be preparing ourselves for the tragic hour when God may set us aside as so-called evangelicals and raise up another movement to keep New Testament Christianity alive in the earth. Say not, "We be children of Abraham. God is able of these stones to raise up children unto Abraham."

### The Imperative of Possessing the Gifts of the Spirit

The truth of the matter is that the Scriptures plainly imply the imperative of possessing the gifts of the Spirit. Paul urges that we both "covet" and "desire" spiritual gifts (1 Cor. 12:32; 14:1). It does not appear to be an optional matter with us but rather a scriptural mandate to those who have been filled with the Spirit.

But I must also add a word of caution.

The various spiritual gifts are not equally valuable, as Paul so carefully explained.

Certain brethren have magnified one gift out of 17 out of all proportion. Among these brethren there have been and are many godly souls, but the general moral results of this teaching have nevertheless not been good.

In practice it has resulted in much shameless exhibitionism, a tendency to depend upon experiences instead of upon Christ and often a lack of ability to distinguish the works of the flesh from the operations of the Spirit.

Those who deny that the gifts are for us today and those who insist upon making a hobby of one gift are both wrong, and we are all suffering the consequences of their errors.

Today there is no reason for our remaining longer in doubt. We have every right to expect our Lord to grant to His Church the spiritual gifts which He has never in fact taken away from us, but which we are failing to receive only because of our error or unbelief.

It is more than possible that God is even now imparting the gifts of the Spirit to whomsoever He can and in whatever measure He can as His conditions are met even imperfectly. Otherwise the torch of truth would flicker out and die.

Clearly, however, we have yet to see what God would do for His Church if we would all throw ourselves down before Him with an open Bible and cry, "Behold Thy servant, Lord! Be it unto me even as Thou wilt."

Today there is no reason for our remaining longer in doubt. We have every right to expect our Lord to grant to His Church the spiritual gifts which He has never in fact taken away from us, but which we are failing to receive only because of our error of unbelief.

A. W. Tozer

## FOUR

# Brimming over
# with the
# Spirit

Almost all Christians want to be *full* of the Spirit.
Only a few want to be filled with the Spirit.

But how can a Christian know the fullness of the
Spirit unless he has known the experience of being
filled?

It would, however, be useless to tell anyone how
to be filled with the Spirit unless he first believes
that he can be. No one can hope for something he is
not convinced is the will of God for him and within
the bounds of scriptural provision.

Before the question "How can I be filled?" has any
validity the seeker after God *must be sure that the
experience of being filled is actually possible.* The
man who is not sure can have no ground of
expectation. Where there is not expectation there

can be no faith, and where there is no faith the inquiry is meaningless.

The doctrine of the Spirit as it relates to the believer has over the last half century been shrouded in a mist such as lies upon a mountain in stormy weather. A world of confusion has surrounded this truth. The children of God have been taught contrary doctrines from the same texts, warned, threatened and intimidated until they instinctively recoil from every mention of the Bible teaching concerning the Holy Spirit.

This confusion has not come by accident. An enemy has done this. Satan knows that Spiritless evangelicalism is as deadly as Modernism or heresy, and he has done everything in his power to prevent us from enjoying our true Christian heritage.

### The Holy Spirit Is Our Cloud by Day, Our Fire by Night

A church without the Spirit is as helpless as Israel might have been in the wilderness if the fiery cloud had deserted them. The Holy Spirit is our cloud by day and our fire by night. Without Him we only wander aimlessly about the desert.

That is what we today are surely doing. We have divided ourselves into little ragged groups, each one running after a will-o'-the-wisp or firefly in the mistaken notion that we are following the Shekinah. It is not only desirable that the cloudy pillar should begin to glow again. It is imperative.

The Church can have light only as it is full of the

Spirit, and it can be full only as the members that compose it are filled individually. Furthermore, no one can be filled until he is convinced that being filled is a part of the total plan of God in redemption; that nothing is added or extra, nothing strange or queer, but a proper and spiritual operation of God, based upon and growing out of the work of Christ in atonement.

The inquirer must be sure to the point of conviction. He must believe that the whole thing is normal and right. He must believe that God wills that he be anointed with a horn of fresh oil beyond and in addition to all the ten thousand blessings he may already have received from the good hand of God.

Until he is so convinced I recommend that he take time out to fast and pray and meditate upon the Scriptures. Faith comes from the Word of God. Suggestion, exhortation or the psychological effect of the testimony of others who may have been filled will not suffice.

Unless he is persuaded from the Scriptures he should not press the matter nor allow himself to fall victim to the emotional manipulators intent upon forcing the issue. God is wonderfully patient and understanding and will wait for the slow heart to catch up with the truth. In the meantime, the seeker should be calm and confident. In due time God will lead him through the Jordan. Let him not break loose and run ahead. Too many have done so, only to bring disaster upon their Christian lives.

After a man is convinced that he can be filled with

the Spirit he *must desire to be*. To the interested
inquirer I ask these questions: Are you sure that you
want to be possessed by a Spirit Who, while He is
pure and gentle and wise and loving, will yet insist
upon being Lord of your life? Are you sure you want
your personality to be taken over by One Who will
require obedience to the written Word? Who will
not tolerate any of the self-sins in your life: self-love,
self-indulgence? Who will not permit you to strut or
boast or show off? Who will take the direction of
your life away from you and will reserve the
sovereign right to test you and discipline you? Who
will strip away from you many loved objects which
secretly harm your soul?

### God ... Demands All or Nothing

Unless you can answer an eager "Yes" to these
questions you do not want to be filled. You may
want the thrill or the victory or the power, but you
do not really want to be filled with the Spirit. Your
desire is little more than a feeble wish and is not
pure enough to please God, Who demands all or
nothing.

Again I ask: Are you sure you *need to be filled*
with the Spirit? Tens of thousands of Christians—
laymen, preachers, missionaries—manage to get on
somehow without having had a clear experience of
being filled. That Spiritless labor can lead only to
tragedy in the day of Christ is something the average
Christian seems to have forgotten. But how about
you?

Perhaps your doctrinal bias is away from belief in the crisis of the Spirit's filling. Very well, look at the fruit of such doctrine. What is your life producing? You are doing religious work, preaching, singing, writing, promoting, but what is the *quality* of your work? True; you received the Spirit at the moment of conversion, but is it also true that you are ready without a further anointing to resist temptation, obey the Scriptures, understand the truth, live victoriously, die in peace and meet Christ without embarrassment at His coming?

If, on the other hand, your soul cries out for God, for the living God, and your dry and empty heart despairs of living a normal Christian life without a further anointing, then I ask you: Is your desire all-absorbing? Is it the biggest thing in your life? Does it crowd out every common religious activity and fill you with an acute longing that can only be described as the pain of desire? If your heart cries "Yes" to these questions you may be on your way to a spiritual breakthrough that will transform your whole life.

It is in the preparation for receiving the Spirit's anointing that most Christians fail. Probably no one was ever filled without first having gone through a period of deep soul disturbance and inward turmoil. When we find ourselves entering this state the temptation is to panic and draw back. Satan exhorts us to take it easy lest we make shipwreck of the faith, and dishonor the Lord that bought us.

Of course he cares nothing for us nor for our Lord.

His purpose is to keep us weak and unarmed in a day of conflict. And millions of believers accept his hypocritical lies as gospel truth and go back to their caves like the prophets of Obadiah to feed on bread and water.

### Before There Can Be Fullness
### There Must Be Emptiness

Before there can be fullness there must be emptiness. Before God can fill us with Himself we must first be emptied of ourselves. It is this emptying that brings the painful disappointment and despair of self of which so many persons have complained just prior to their new and radiant experience.

There must come a total of self-devaluation, a death to all things without us and within us, or there can never be real filling with the Holy Spirit.

> The dearest idol I have known,
>> Whate'er that idol be,
> Help me to tear it from Thy throne,
>> And worship only Thee.

We sing this glibly enough, but we cancel out our prayer by our refusal to surrender the very idol of which we sing. To give up our last idol is to plunge ourselves into a state of inward loneliness which no gospel meeting, no fellowship with other Christians, can ever cure. For this reason most Christians play it safe and settle for a life of compromise. They have some of God, to be sure, but not all; and God has some of them, but not all. And so they live their

tepid lives and try to disguise with bright smiles and
snappy choruses the deep spiritual destitution within them.

One thing should be made crystal clear: The soul's
journey through the dark night is not a meritorious
one. The suffering and the loneliness do not make a
man dear to God nor earn the horn of oil for which
he yearns. We cannot buy anything from God.
Everything comes out of His goodness on the
grounds of Christ's redeeming blood and is a free
gift, with no strings attached.

What the soul agony does is to break up the fallow
ground, empty the vessel, detach the heart from
earthly interests and focus the attention upon God.

All that has gone before is by way of soul
preparation for the divine act of infilling. The
infilling itself is not a complicated thing. While I
shy away from "how to" formulas in spiritual
things, I believe the answer to the question "How
can I be filled?" may be answered in four words, all
of them active verbs. They are these: *(1) surrender,
(2) ask, (3) obey, (4) believe.*

*Surrender:* "I beseech you therefore, brethren, by
the mercies of God, that ye present your bodies a
living sacrifice, holy, acceptable unto God, which is
your reasonable service. And be not conformed to
this world: but be ye transformed by the renewing of
your mind, that ye may prove what is that good, and
acceptable, and perfect, will of God" (Rom. 12:1, 2).

*Ask:* "If ye then, being evil, know how to give
good gifts unto your children: how much more shall

your heavenly Father give the Holy Spirit to them that ask him?" (Luke 11:13).

*Obey:* "We are his witnesses of these things; and so is also the Holy Ghost, whom God hath given to them that obey him" (Acts 5:32).

Complete and ungrudging obedience to the will of God is absolutely indispensable to the reception of the Spirit's anointing. As we wait before God we should reverently search the Scriptures and listen for the voice of gentle stillness to learn what our heavenly Father expects of us. Then, trusting in His enabling, we should obey to the best of our ability and understanding.

*Believe:* "This only would I learn of you, Received ye the Spirit by the works of the law, or by the hearing of faith?" (Gal. 3:2).

## True Faith Invariably Brings a Witness

While the infilling of the Spirit is received by faith and only by faith, let us beware of that imitation faith which is no more than a mental assent to truth. It has been a source of great disappointment to multitudes of seeking souls. True faith invariably brings a witness.

But what is that witness? It is nothing physical, vocal nor psychical. The Spirit never commits Himself to the flesh. The only witness He gives is a subjective one, known to the individual alone. The Spirit announces Himself to the deep, inner spirit of the man. The flesh profiteth nothing, but the believing heart knows. *Holy, holy, holy.*

One last thing: Neither in the Old Testament nor in the New, nor in Christian testimony as found in the writings of the saints as far as my knowledge goes was any believer ever filled with the Holy Spirit *who did not know he had been filled.* Neither was anyone filled *who did not know when he was filled.* And *no one was ever filled gradually.*

Behind these three trees many half-hearted souls have tried to hide like Adam from the presence of the Lord, but they are not good enough hiding places: The man who does not know when he was filled was never filled (though of course it is possible to forget the date). And the man who hopes to be filled gradually will never be filled at all.

In my sober judgment the relation of the Spirit to the believer is the most vital question the church faces today. The problems raised by Christian existentialism or neo-orthodoxy are nothing by comparison with this most critical one. Ecumenicity, eschatalogical theories—none of these things deserve consideration until every believer can give an affirmative answer to the question, "Have ye received the Holy Ghost since ye believed?"

And it might easily be that after we have been filled with the Spirit we will find to our delight that the very filling itself has solved the other problems for us.

It is very important to listen to God. A man came to see me. He talked for an hour about his troubles. Next week he came again and I talked to him for an hour. The next week he came to see me again. I said to him, "The first time you talked for an hour. The second time I talked for an hour. Now let us give everyone a chance to talk. Let us be silent and let God tell us what He wants to say." After an hour of silence God was able to show this man how to solve his problems.

**Paul Tournier, Ph.D.**

# FIVE

# Touching
# Heaven
# in Prayer

Many prayer meetings are being called these days. And no wonder, for the need is great. But if my observation is correct much effort is wasted; very little comes of them.

The reason is that motives are not sound.

Too many praying persons seek to use prayer as a means to ends that are not wholly pure. Prayer is often conceived to be little more than a technique for self-advancement, a heavenly method of achieving earthly success.

Every kind of personal religious project these days is being made the object of prayer.

Some of these projects are unscriptural, or at least extrascriptural, and many of them have no higher motive than to relieve the promoter of the unpleasant task of earning an honest living and to enable him to float about the world at the expense of the hard-pressed saints. Yet he may circularize his mailing list begging for the prayers of God's people, and call prolonged prayer meetings to try to gain the blessing of God upon activities God did not originate and will not own.

The Scriptures are very clear about the place of prayer in the economy of God.

Prayer was practiced by every believing soul from righteous Abel to John the Revelator, and it has been the vital breath of the church through the long centuries of her struggle on earth. Of prayer, properly understood, hardly too much can be said. This piece deals with prayer that is improperly understood and wrongly used.

The Scriptures are clear about the potency of prayer.

"The effectual fervent prayer of a righteous man," wrote the inspired James, "availeth much." With this the whole Bible and Christian experience agree: *Prayer is effective.* When it is not answered something is wrong.

The same apostle who affirmed the effective power of prayer admitted also that prayer is sometimes ineffective: "Ye ask, and receive not, because ye ask amiss, that ye may consume it upon your lusts."

In spite of the difficulties surrounding prayer it is still the highest activity in which a human being can engage. Knowing all about prayer and all about people our Lord said, "Men ought always to pray, and not to faint."

### Reasons for Failure

This effort to discover the reasons for our leanness in prayer is intended not to discourage praying but to find the causes back of our ineffectual prayers and remove them. There is no virtue in continuing grimly to pray on when there are factors present that make our prayers of no effect. We should pray on, but we must pray aright or our prayers will continue to be fruitless.

We need only to listen to the average prayer to discover what is wrong.

Even in specially called prayer meetings where, it would be supposed, the most spiritual persons in a community are present, many of the prayers are little more than pious monologues on current events. They are suggested by the newscasts rather than inspired by the Spirit. They cover the earth like clouds without rain, promising much and delivering little.

To pray effectively we must want what God wants—that and only that is to pray in the will of God. And no petition made in the will of God was ever refused. "This is the confidence that we have in him, that, if we ask anything according to his will, he heareth us: and if we know that he hear us, whatsoever we ask, we know that we have the petitions that we desired of him" (1 John 5:14, 15)

Furthermore, to pray effectively we must pray

within the context of the world situation *as God
sees it*. Not what the world thinks about itself
should influence us, but what God thinks about the
world.

Prayer that slavishly follows the day-by-day de-
velopment of world news may quite easily be
wasted. Most world events as reported by various
news media are like ping-pong balls being batted
back and forth. They are lively enough, they make
an attention-getting racket, but they lack significance.

Surely the God Who presides over history knows
how few things matter. But He knows also what
things *do* matter; and if we are spiritual enough to
hear His voice He will lead us to engage in the kind
of praying that will be effective.

For some years I have had a growing conviction
that the world situation as God sees it presents two
major goals to be reached by praying people, two
objects at which to aim our prayers.

One is *that the glory of God be seen again among
men*, and the other *that the church be delivered
from her present Babylonian captivity*.

For several generations the evangelical Christian
world has run on hearsay. We look back pensively
to the Fathers who met God in brilliant and satisfying encounter. We quote them lovingly and try to
draw what spiritual nourishment we can from the
knowledge that the High and Lofty One once
manifested Himself to wondering men. We pore
over the record of His self-revelations to men like

Abraham, Jacob, Moses and Isaiah. We read with longing hearts how once "the place was shaken where they were assembled together; and they were all filled with the Holy Ghost, and they spake the word of God with boldness." We read the stories of Edwards and Finney, and our hearts yearn to see again a shining forth of the glory of God.

### Our Obligation

I believe we are under positive spiritual obligation to pray effectively till the present veil is torn away and the face of God is seen again by believing men.

The second object at which our prayers should be aimed is the restoration of the spiritual life of the church. We must continue to pray that she should cease her disgraceful fornication with the world and return to her first love and her true Lord. Her living has degenerated, her tastes have declined, her standards have sunk to the bottom. Nothing short of a radical reformation can save her. Only those with anointed eyes are able to see her plight and only those with Spirit-filled hearts can intercede for her effectively.

Now, even if we concentrate upon these vitally important items it is still entirely possible to ask amiss and gain nothing but leanness and utter disappointment. Why?

The problem is *self*. Selfishness is never so exquisitely selfish as when it is on its knees. Self is the serpent in the garden, the golden wedge in the tent of Achan, and it renders every prayer ineffective until it is identified and repudiated.

Self turns what would otherwise be a pure and powerful prayer into a weak and ineffective one.

I may, for instance, pray earnestly for the glory of God to be manifested to this generation of men, and spoil the whole thing by my secret hope that I may be the one through whom He manifests the glory.

I may cry loudly to God that the church be restored to her New Testament splendor, and secretly dream that I may be the one to lead her in; thus I block the work of the Spirit by my impure motive. My hidden desire for a share of the glory prevents God from hearing me. So self, all bold and shameless, follows me to the altar, kneels with me in prayer and destroys my prayer before it is uttered.

It is possible to want the walls of Jerusalem rebuilt, but to want to be known as the Nehemiah who rebuilt them. It is possible to want the prophets of Baal defeated, but to dream of being the Elijah who stands dramatically on the mount to call down the fire for all the world to see. My strong desire for a new reformation within the church may be rendered void by my secret desire to be known as another Luther.

Did you ever pray that the armies of the Lord might win in the mighty struggle against the flesh and the devil and catch yourself daydreaming about riding up front in the open car when the grateful church stages a tickertape parade to welcome the returning heroes?

If you are a minister, have you ever dreamed of a sea of eager faces hanging on your every word?

If you are a Christian businessman, have you ever let your mind wander over your mighty prayers for success in business, the dramatic answer, the proud testimony, maybe the book with your picture on it?

Then you know what it is to be hit where it hurts worst; you know what it is to be attacked where you are most defenseless.

Too often we pray for right things but desire the answer for wrong reasons, one reason being a desire to gain a reputation among the saints. Long after every hope of getting on the cover of *Time* magazine has ebbed away from our hearts we may still harbor the unconfessed desire to get on the cover of *Christian Life*. That is, if the world will not appreciate our sterling worth, then the church will! If we cannot enjoy the reputation of being a great statesman or actor or ballplayer we will settle for a big reputation as an unusual Christian. That is to desire flesh instead of manna; and God may send leanness to our souls as a result.

### The Peril of Prayer

Nothing is so vital as prayer, yet a reputation for being a mighty prayer warrior is probably the most perilous of all reputations to have. No form of selfishness is so deeply and dangerously sinful as that which glories in being a man of prayer. It comes near to being self-worship; and that while in the very act of worshiping God.

What then shall we do?

We must deny self, take up the cross and count ourselves expendable.

We must cease to exercise the world's judgments and try to think God's thoughts after Him.

We must reckon ourselves dead to gain and glory and allow ourselves to become inextricably involved with the cross of Christ and the high honor of God.

Then our prayers will be something like this: O God, let Thy glory be revealed once more to men: through me if it please Thee, or without me or apart from me, it matters not. Restore Thy church to the place of moral beauty that becomes her as the Bride of Christ: through me, or apart from me; only let this prayer be answered. O God, honor whom Thou wilt. Let me be used or overlooked or ignored or forgotten.

Prayer is still the greatest power on earth if it is practiced in the true fear of God. It is our solemn obligation to see that it is so practiced.

Neither in the Old Testament nor in the New, nor in Christian testimony as found in the writings of the saints ... was any believer filled with the Holy Spirit who did not know he had been filled. Neither was anyone filled who did not know when he was filled. And no one was ever filled gradually.

A. W. Tozer

# SIX

# Favorite Themes from Tozer

### How Do You Measure Success?

Our Lord died an apparent failure, discredited by the leaders of established religion, rejected by society and forsaken by His friends. The man who ordered Him to the cross was the successful statesman whose hand the ambitious hack-politician kissed. It took the resurrection to demonstrate how gloriously Christ had triumphed and how tragically the governor had failed.

Yet today the professed church seems to have learned nothing. We are still seeing as men see and judging after the manner of man's judgment. How much eager-beaver religious work is done out of a carnal desire to make good. How many man hours for prayer are wasted beseeching God to bless projects that are geared to glorification of little men. How much sacred money is poured out upon men who, in spite of their tear-in-the-voice appeals, nevertheless seek only to make a fair show in the flesh.

The true Christian should turn away from all this. Especially should ministers of the gospel search their own hearts and look deep into their inner motives. No man is worthy to succeed until he is willing to fail. No man is morally worthy of success in religious activities until he is willing that the honor of succeeding should go to another if God so wills. . . .

God will allow His servant to succeed when he has learned that success does not make him dearer to God nor more valuable in the total scheme of things. We cannot buy God's favor with crowds or converts to new missionaries sent out or Bibles distributed. All these things can be accomplished without the help of the Holy Spirit. A good personality and a shrewd knowledge of human nature is all that any man needs to be a success in religious circles today.

Our great honor lies in being just what Jesus was and is. To be accepted by those who accept Him, rejected by all who reject Him, loved by those who love Him and hated by everyone that hates Him. What greater glory could come to any man?*

*Born After Midnight, pp. 58–59, by A. W. Tozer © 1959 by Christian Publications, Inc., Camp Hill, PA. Used by permission.

### The Mercy of God Speaks Louder
### Than the Voice of Justice

All offenses against God will either be forgiven or avenged—we can take our choice. All offenses against God, against ourselves, against humanity, against human life—all offenses will be either forgiven or avenged.

What a terrible thing for men and women to get old and have no prospect, no gracious promise for the long eternity before them.

But how beautiful to come up like a ripe shock of corn and know that the Father's house is open, the doors are wide open, and the Father waits to receive His children one after another!

Some years ago one of our national Christian brothers from the land of Thailand gave his testimony in my hearing. He told what it had meant in his life and for his future when the missionaries came with the good news of the gospel of Christ.

He described the godly life of one of the early missionaries and then said: "He is in the Father's house now."

He told of one of the missionary ladies and the love of Christ she had displayed, and then said: "She is in the Father's house now."

What a vision for a humble Christian who only a generation before had been a pagan, worshiping idols and spirits—and now because of grace and mercy he talks about the Father's house as though it was just a step away, across the street.

This is the gospel of Christ—the kind of Christianity I believe in. What a joy to discover that God is not mad at us and that we are His children— because Jesus died for us, because the blood of Jesus speaketh better things than the blood of Abel. What a blessing to find out that the mercy of God speaks louder than the voice of justice. What a hope that makes it possible for the Lord's people to lie down quietly when the time comes and whisper, "Father, I am coming home!"*

## One Cannot Fight Sin with Sin

Some time ago I heard a prayer uttered by a servant of God who was deeply grieved over the lack of spirituality in the church of which he was the pastor. His prayer was, "O Lord, let me not become vexed with the ways of my people."

Always it is more important that we retain a right spirit toward others than that we bring them to our way of thinking, even if our way is right.

Satan has achieved a real victory when he succeeds in getting us to react in an unspiritual way toward sins and failures in our brethren. We cannot fight sin with sin or draw men to God by frowning at them in fleshly anger. "For the wrath of man worketh not the righteousness of God."

Often acts done in a spirit of religious irritation have consequences far beyond anything we could

*Echoes from Eden, pp. 50–51, by A. W. Tozer © 1981 by Christian Publications, Inc., Camp Hill, PA. Used by permission.

have guessed. Moses allowed himself to become vexed with Israel and in a fit of pique smote the rock. With the same stroke he closed the land of promise against him for the rest of his life.

I heard of a certain man of God who had been greatly used in praying for the sick with the natural result that he was often called out at very inopportune times and under circumstances that were anything but pleasant. Once when sent for in the middle of the night he threw himself across the bed and complained to God for the lack of consideration the call evinced. That was the end for him. Thereafter no one was ever delivered in answer to his prayer, even though he sought with many tears to capture again the gift he had lost.

It is quite natural, and even spiritual, to feel sorrow and heaviness when we see the professed followers of Christ walking in the ways of the world. And our first impulse may easily be to go straight to them and upbraid them indignantly. But such methods are seldom successful. The heat in our spirit may not be from the Holy Ghost, and if it is not then it can very well do more harm than good.

In this as in everything else Christ is our perfect example. A prayerful, face-down meditation on the life of Christ will show us how to oppose with kindness and reprove with charity. And the power of the Holy Spirit within us will enable us to follow His blessed example.*

*Of God and Men, pp. 92–94, by A. W. Tozer © 1960 by Christian Publications, Inc., Camp Hill, PA. Used by permission.

### *Who Is Lord of Your Life?*

When we come to the question of our own relationship with God through the merits of our Lord Jesus Christ, we come to one of those areas which in a supreme degree is truly a matter of life and death.

This is so desperately a matter of importance for every human being who comes into the world that I first become indignant, and then I become sad, when I try to give spiritual counsel to a person who looks me in the eye and tells me: "Well, I am trying to make up my mind if I should accept Christ or not."

Such a person gives absolutely no indication that he realizes he is talking about the most important decision he can make in his lifetime—a decision to get right with God, to believe in the eternal Son, the Savior, to become a disciple, an obedient witness to Jesus Christ as Lord.

How can any man or woman, lost and undone, sinful and wretched, alienated from God, stand there and intimate that the death and resurrection of Jesus Christ and God's revealed plan of salvation do not take priority over some of life's other decisions? . . .

We know about His Divine Person, we know that He is the Lamb of God Who suffered and died in our place. We know all about His credentials. Yet we let Him stand outside on the steps like some poor timid fellow who is hoping he can find a job.

We look Him over, then read a few more devotional verses, and ask: "What do you think, Mabel? Do you think we ought to accept Him? I really wonder if we should accept Him?"

My friend, look: doesn't that proud human know that the Christ he is putting off is the Christ of God, the eternal Son Who holds the world in His hands?

Why this One Who patiently waits for our human judgment is the One Who holds the stars in His hands. He is the Savior and Lord and head over all things to the Church. It will be at His word that the graves shall give us their dead, and the dead shall come forth, alive forevermore. At His word, the fire shall burst loose and burn up the earth and the heavens and the stars and the planets shall be swept away like a garment.

He is the One; the Mighty One!*

### Love Not the World

Every faithful pastor can tell you, with great sorrow and concern, the stories of young people and men and women who walked away from the church and straight Bible-teaching and warm Christian fellowship to have their own way. When the old nature stirred, they turned their backs on God and walked away. They went into questionable marriages. They went into worldly alliances. They took jobs in which there was no chance to please and glorify God. They went back into the world.

---

*Christ the Eternal Son, pp. 121–122, by A. W. Tozer © 1982 by Christian Publications, Inc., Camp Hill, PA. Used by permission.

Now, they did not walk out of the house of God because they did not want God—but because they found something they wanted more than God! God has given men and women the opportunity for free will and free choices—and some are determined to have what they want most.

The rich young ruler made his decision on the basis of what he wanted most in life. The last thing we know about him is the fact that he turned from Jesus and walked away. He was sorry about it and sorrowful, because he had great earthly possessions. But Jesus looked upon him as he walked away and Jesus was sorrowful, too.

I admit that there are parents who counsel me about the danger of losing young people from our church life because I am faithful in preaching against this present world and the worldly system in which we live.

I can only say that I am concerned and I will stand and cry at the door when they decide to go, but I will not be guilty of deceiving them. I refuse to deceive and damn them by teaching that you can be a Christian and love this present world, for you cannot.

Yes, you can be a hypocrite and love the world.

You can be a deceived ruler in the religious system and love the world.

You can be a cheap, snobbish, modern Christian and love the world.

But you cannot be a genuine Bible Christian and

love the world. It would grieve me to stand alone on this principle, but I will not lie to you about it.*

### The Holy Spirit Is Not Enthusiasm

I think you will agree with me when I say that many people are confused about the Spirit of God. The Holy Spirit, for instance, is not enthusiasm. Some people get enthusiasm, and they imagine it is the Holy Spirit. Some who can get all worked up over a song imagine that this is the Spirit, but this does not necessarily follow. Some of these same people go out and live just like the sinful world— but the Holy Spirit never enters a man and then lets him live just like the world that hates God. That is the reason most people don't want to be filled with the Holy Spirit—they want to live the way they want to live and to merely have the Holy Spirit as a bit of something extra.

I tell you that the Holy Spirit will not be just an addition. The Holy Spirit must be Lord, or He will not come at all.

The Holy Spirit is a Person. He is not enthusiasm. He is not courage. He is not energy. He is not the personification of all good qualities like Jack Frost is the personification of cold weather. Actually the Holy Spirit is not the personification of anything. He is a person, just the same as you are a person, and

*The Tozer Pulpit, Vol. 6, pp. 56–57, by A. W. Tozer © 1975 by Christian Publications, Inc., Camp Hill, PA. Used by permission.

He has all the qualities of a person. . . . He can hear, speak, desire, grieve, and rejoice. He is a Person.

The Holy Spirit can communicate with you and can love you. He can be grieved when you resist and ignore Him. He can be quenched as any friend can be shut up if you turn on him when he is in your home as a guest. Of course, he will be hushed into hurt silence if you wound him, and we can wound the Holy Spirit.

Now, let us consider the question, "Who is the Holy Spirit?"

Well, the historic Christian church said that the Holy Spirit is God. . . .

Yes, the Holy Spirit is God, and the most important thing is that the Holy Spirit is present now. There is unseen deity present. I cannot bring Him to you; I can only tell you that He is here. I can tell you that He is present in our midst, a knowing, feeling personality.*

## Love: The Willed Tendency of the Heart

How can the sincere Christian fulfill the scriptural command to love God with all his heart and his neighbor as himself?

Of all the emotions of which the soul is capable, love is by far the freest, the most unreasoning, the one least likely to spring up at the call of duty or

*When He Is Come, pp. 49–54, by A. W. Tozer © 1968 by Christian Publications, Inc., Camp Hill, PA. Used by permission.

obligation, and surely the one that will not come at the command of another.

No law has ever been passed that can compel one moral being to love another, for by the very nature of it love must be voluntary. No one can be coerced or frightened into loving anyone. Love just does not come that way!

The love the Bible enjoins is not the love of feeling: it is the love of willing, the "willed tendency" of the heart.

God never intended that such a being as man should be the plaything of his feelings. The emotional life is a proper and noble part of the total personality, but it is, by its very nature, of secondary importance. Religion lies in the will, and so does righteousness. The only good that God recognizes is a willed good; the only valid holiness is a willed holiness.

It should be a cheering thought that before God every man is what he wills to be. The first requirement in conversion is a rectified will. To meet the requirements of love toward God the soul need but will to love and the miracle begins to blossom like the budding of Aaron's rod!*

### Everything Is Wrong Until God Sets It Right

"Worship is to feel in your heart and express in some appropriate manner a humbling but delightful

---

*Renewed Day by Day, July 22, by A. W. Tozer © 1980 by Christian Publications, Inc., Camp Hill, PA. Used by permission.

sense of admiring awe and astonished wonder and overpowering love in the presence of that most ancient Mystery, that Majesty which philosophers call the First Cause but which we call Our Father Which Art in Heaven."

Though sometimes considered iconoclastic, Tozer explained his skepticism: "I guess my philosophy is that everything is wrong until God sets it right."

"Every Spirit-led saint knows there are times when he is held by an inward pressure to one chapter, or even a verse, for days at a time while he wrestles with God till some truth does its work within him.

"I refuse to allow any man to put his glasses on me and force me to see everything in his light. I love all God's children and rarely try to learn which side of the old controversy they are on.

"Our Lord commands us to pray the Lord of harvest that He will send forth laborers into His harvest field," he said. "But we are overlooking that no one can be a worker who is not first a worshiper. Labor that does not spring out of worship is futile."

Near the end of his life, Tozer expressed his view about God simply: "I have found God cordial and generous and in every way easy to live with."*

---

*Lessons from a 20th Century Prophet, by David Enlow, Moody Monthly.

# Addendum

The following interview with
A. W. Tozer appeared in the August 1954 issue of *Christian Life*
magazine. Nothing could more
clearly illustrate how prophetic
Tozer was in his discernment of
the spiritual renewal we now are
seeing throughout evangelical
Christianity in the historic denominations as well as in the Roman
Catholic church.

# Can Evangelicalism Be Saved?

## by David Enlow

*A. W. Tozer, evangelicalism's penetrating analyst, shakes a stern finger at today and traces a possible bright tomorrow.*

"Why aren't we seeing the power of God demonstrated today as in the first century?"

This and other equally pointed questions asked frequently in evangelical Christian circles augur well for the future of evangelicalism, in the opinion of one of America's staunchest champions of the "deeper life."

Dr. A. W. Tozer, outstanding spokesman of the Christian and Missionary Alliance, author of *The Pursuit of God* and other books, editor of *The Alliance Weekly*, and pastor of the Southside C&MA

Church in Chicago, answered questions for *Christian Life* regarding the future of evangelicalism.

In addition to his writing and preaching ministry, Dr. Tozer is heard every Saturday morning in "Talks from a Pastor's Study" over Moody Bible Institute's WMBI. He also has been heard widely in Bible conferences and is recognized by many as one of evangelicalism's most original thinkers.

Question: Dr. Tozer, what significance do you attach to the growing discontent of evangelicals with the present spiritual depth of believers?

Tozer: I believe it is a healthy revolt against the cold textualism characteristic of evangelicalism for a quarter of a century or more. You see, several converging forces met to determine the attitudes and temper of evangelicalism. The strong emphasis on dispensationalism, for instance, which started out to "rightly divide the word of truth" ended up by creating an army of cookie-cutter believers, all repeating each other without any independent thought and without much need for the illumination of the Spirit.

The French naturalist, Faber, told of his starting a number of army worms around the rim of a jar. They followed each other blindly for days, each one dimly seeing the one ahead of him and following without question. After days of getting nowhere, they began one at a time to fall off the edge of the jar and perish. Evangelical leaders, like these army worms, have for decades been following each other around the rim of their own little jars, each one afraid to step aside or hunt any new direction for himself, each slavishly following the other.

And it so happens that the emphasis has been away from the "deeper life," the Spirit-filled life, the life hid with Christ in God. The spiritual content of evangelicalism has been lowered. But, encouragingly, some people are growing discontented and are demanding bread instead of a stone. If there are enough of such people and if they speak out, it could mean healthy revival in the church of Christ.

*Question:* You mentioned that the current emphasis is away from the "deeper life." Dr. Tozer, exactly how would you define "deeper life"?

*Tozer:* It means a spiritual life with an intensity of purity and fruitfulness far in advance of that of the average Christian life. It involves complete separation from the world, not only in practice but in spirit, and a full devotion to God without reservation.

*Question:* How is this "deeper life" obtained?

*Tozer:* I believe it is the result of a crisis rather than a slow growth in grace. The emotional content of this crisis varies with the individual. However, the main point is not the degree of emotional experience, but the fact that the experience actually has taken place.

A fine Old Testament example may be found in the life of Jacob. He met God in the waste, howling wilderness. His encounter was real and to some degree satisfying. Then after wandering for 20 years, during which time he was up and down, sometimes victorious but mostly in defeat, he met God again at Peniel. This second crisis resulted in a complete moral and spiritual transformation that stayed with him for the remainder of his days.

Question: Dr. Tozer, what specific steps would you suggest for the earnest seeker after the "deeper life"?

Tozer: I have never been much for "steps" in the Christian life, though they may be useful to some people. For the most part, my method has been simply to plunge in on the promises of God and let God take care of the "steps." I would, however, make a few recommendations to anyone seeking a more satisfying and more God-possessed life than he now enjoys.

First, determine to take the whole thing in dead earnest. Too many of us play at Christianity. We wear salvation as a kind of convention badge admitting us into the circle of the elect, but rarely stop to focus our whole lives seriously on God's claims upon us.

Second, throw yourself out recklessly upon God. Give up everything and prepare yourself to surrender even unto death all of your ambitions, plans and possessions. And I mean this quite literally. You should not be satisfied with the mere technical aspect of surrender but press your case upon God in determined prayer until a crisis has taken place within your life and there has been an actual transfer of everything from yourself to God.

Third, take a solemn vow never to claim any

honor or glory or praise for anything you are or have or do. See to it that God gets all honor, all the time.

Fourth, determine not to defend yourself against detractors and persecutors. Put your reputation in God's hands and leave it there.

Fifth, mortify the flesh with the affections and lusts. Every believer has been judicially put to death with Christ, but this is not enough for present victory. Freedom from the power of the flesh will come only when we have by faith and self-discipline made such death an actuality. Real death to self is a painful thing and tends to reduce a man in his own eyes and humble him into the dust. Not many follow this rugged way, but those who do are the exemplary Christians.

*Question:* What do you feel would do most to awaken the church from its complacency?

*Tozer:* A great Christian of nearly 300 years ago, Nicholas Herman of Lorraine said that in his early Christian life he determined to cut through the tangle of religious means and "nourish his heart on high thoughts of God." I have always treasured that expression.

A cultivation of God through prayer, humble soul-searching and avid feasting upon the Scriptures would go far to awaken the church. As long as God is considered to be very much like the rest of us, except a little higher and a little greater, there won't be any great amount of holy fear among church people.

In my opinion, the great single need of the

moment is that light-hearted superficial religionists
be struck down with a vision of God high and lifted
up, with His train filling the temple. The holy art of
worship seems to have passed away like the Shekinah glory from the tabernacle. As a result, we are left
to our own devices and forced to make up the lack
of spontaneous worship by bringing in countless
cheap and tawdry activities to hold the attention of
the church people.

*Question:* Where is evangelicalism falling farthest
short today?

*Tozer:* I believe current evangelicalism is falling
short in its attitude toward God, its attitude toward
the world and its attitude toward sin.

I have been hurt and shocked continuously by the
levity displayed toward God by many supposed
followers of Christ. Worldliness has become epi-
demic in evangelical circles. Although we still
condemn worldliness, we have redefined it to mean
something different from what it meant a generation
ago. We are so afraid of being narrow that we have
opened our doors to worldliness. Of course, this
leads only to spiritual tragedy for everyone.

*Question:* Do you feel that we are standing still or
retrogressing?

*Tozer:* In my opinion we have been retrogressing
rapidly during the last 20 years. That retrogression
has been speeded up tremendously since World War
II. It would not surprise me if there should yet come
a sharp division in evangelical ranks, springing not
out of doctrinal differences so much as out of

methods, practices, objectives, techniques and particularly out of the difference in spiritual attitudes.

Popular evangelicalism has been selling out to the worldly spirit and worldly methods to a point where Hollywood now has more influence than Jerusalem ever had. Youth take for their examples not the saints of old but the stars of today. The chaste dignity and sparkling purity of true Christianity has been displaced by a cheap hillbillyism wholly unworthy of our Lord Jesus Christ.

*Question:* Are there any encouraging signs on the spiritual horizon?

*Tozer:* Yes, most encouraging is the increasing number of dissatisfied and dissenting believers thoroughly sick of the cheap and tawdry religion currently promoted in the name of New Testament Christianity. These believers might turn out to be the new prophets to our day. They are numerically in the minority, but their power might yet prove to be great enough to bring a change for the better among the gospel churches, unless—as stated before—God is forced to desert the great mass of worldly Christians and raise up something nearer to His own heart.

*Question:* What, in your opinion, comprises genuine revival?

*Tozer:* Revival may occur on three levels. There is community revival such as under the preaching of Jonathan Edwards in New England and Charles Finney in the Midwest. These revivals jumped over denominational lines and affected whole towns and cities. The temper and attitude of the people were radically changed. The moral standards were raised and the churches prospered spiritually and numerically.

Revival may occur in the local church, too. When a fair percentage of the members of any local church begin to pray more, lead holier lives, love each other more fervently, serve God and their fellow men with greater zeal, and seek to be holy and Christlike, then you have revival on the church level. I am happy to say this does occur sometimes.

And revival may occur in the individual believer's life. Wherever a careless, fleshly Christian suddenly pulls his life together, turns on himself and seeks the face of God in penitence and tears, you have the beginning of a personal revival.

*Question:* In what way can Christian leaders, missionary societies, and other Christian organizations best contribute to genuine revival?

*Tozer:* Let me answer this question in three parts. Christian leaders can help to bring about revival by refusing to pander to the carnal tastes of the religious public and going on a holy crusade for a purified church. If leaders have the courage to follow Christ all the way, they can be a powerful instrument of the Holy Ghost to bring about real revival.

All missionary societies and all missionaries must accept New Testament standards in all things. It is a waste of time and money and human energy to promulgate a decadent Christianity among the heathen. We have no authority to carry anything to the heathen except the message and teaching of the New Testament.

Christian organizations can best contribute to genuine revival by following the methods of the New Testament instead of the methods of big business. Some organizations feel that they can bring about revival by eating and talking. As soon as the subject of revival is brought up, somebody either wants to hold a panel discussion or throw a banquet. Though I admit that I have been after-dinner speaker at many a banquet in my day, I have never been so naive as to believe that a revival would come out of such efforts. Only long, contin-ued, faith-filled, travailing prayer can bring true revival.

*Question:* How would you sum up the subject of evangelicalism and its future?

*Tozer:* The hope for the evangelical forces in America lies with the individual believer, and especially with the individual Christian leader. If enough influential Christians will rethink this whole thing and turn to the New Testament for guidance, there may yet come a new birth of revival among us. These leaders must see that the believer's true ambition should not be success but saintliness. They must see that they are not called to imitate the world, but to renounce it, and that publicity is no substitute for the power of the Holy Ghost.

In addition, they must cease to be afraid of the Holy Spirit. The excesses and vagaries of certain elements in the churches have frightened many of God's people away from the fountain of living waters. Rather than have wild fire, they have chosen to have none of His operations at all. Rather than be mistaken about the operations of the Spirit, they have chosen to have none of His operations at all. They have allowed themselves to be "dispensation-alized" into a state of spiritual vacuity. We must revolt against this Babylonian Captivity. We must have courage to disagree even with big names and famous men, if we can get satisfied no other way. Never forget, God is on the side of the thirsty saint. You do not need to persuade Him to meet you. He is already persuaded. Just dare to trust Him.